CLOUD PHARMACY

Books by Susan Rich

The Alchemist's Kitchen (2010)
Cures Include Travel (2006)
The Cartographer's Tongue / *Poems of the World* (2000)

CLOUD PHARMACY

Susan Rich

For Brandon,
From one
poet to
another.

All best,

10/2/21

WHITE PINE PRESS / BUFFALO, NEW YORK

White Pine Press
P.O. Box 236
Buffalo, New York 14201
www.whitepine.org

Acknowledgments appear on page 91, which constitutes an extension of this copyright page.

Publication of this book was made possible, in part, by grants from Amazon.com and the National Endowment for the Arts, which believes that a great nation deserves great art; and with public funds from the New York State Council on the Arts, a State Agency.

Cover art: "East Bedroom, Hannah Road," photographed by Heinrick Jason Oldhauser. Copyright ©2014 by Heinrick Jason Oldhauser. Used by permission of the artist.

First Edition
Second Printing

ISBN: 978-1-935210-53-5

Printed and bound in the United States of America.

Library of Congress Control Number: 2013942905

I am deeply indebted to the South Grand Poets for their wild laughter, abundant snacks, and late night poetry critiques. Thank you for your continued generosity and unabashed belief in words. I am honored to be one among you: T. Clear, Jeff Crandall, Kathleen Flenniken, Kathryn Hunt, Rosanne Olson, Anne McDuffie, Ted McMahon, Jed Myers, and Peter Pereira.

For providing comments on this book-in-progress, I am grateful beyond words to Kelli Russell Agodon, Annette Spaulding-Convy, and Kathleen Flenniken. Your generous hearts humble and delight me. Friend is too small a word for our connection. Thank you for your generosity of spirit, searing intellect, and lasting affection.

A deep bow to two stellar poets and friends, Christine Deavel and John Marshall, for their labyrinth of love: Open Books: A Poem Emporium. You both guide our community with humor and grace. Thank you for all that you do for American poetry and poets.

And immeasurable gratitude to Jan North for providing a refuge from the city along with an abiding spirit and sharing your pleasure in the visual arts. For super-express service and advice on finding rogue artists, thank you to Maria Gudaitis. For the best cat care ever, the Oscar goes to Sarah Pitzen.

Thank you also to the vision and life work of Arthur Whitely (1916-2013) and the Helene Riaboff Whiteley Center for two residencies that allowed me the time and space needed to do this work. Thank you also to Anam Cara in the West of Ireland for a residency that aided in the completion of this book. And to the poets of Anam Cara: Pippa Little, Kimberly Fahner, Kathryn Stern, and most of all, Angie Vorhies, your creative work, wild stories, and openness to the craft continue to inspire me.

For Booklifters —you know who you are, thank you for the wine and camaraderie of women writers at the Sorrento. To the women poets of Poets on the Coast, your enthusiasm and unbridled joy for poetry and community lift me up every September. I look forward to more adventures.

An abiding appreciation to the organizations that supported this book by providing crucial funding, travel, and space to write in the guise of awards: Artists Trust, Seattle City Artists, and 4Culture. Thank you to Highline Community College for a sabbatical that allowed me the essential element of time.

And from the magic of the internet; deep appreciation goes to Heinrick Jason Oldhauser, photographer extraordinaire for his image, "East Bedroom, Hannah Road." For listening like a pro, thank you to Gina Formea.

Special thanks to Dennis Maloney and Elaine LaMattina for nearly a decade and a half of collaboration.

Finally, a deep familial thank you to Ruby Rich and Mary Peelen for your love, support, and belief in me. It means the world. Thank you to Jeff and Lilly Wasserman my familial unit in Seattle, for taking on the task—with laughter and Golden Gardens.

For Jeff

What makes a photograph a strange invention—with unforeseeable consequences— is that the primary materials are light and time.

—John Berger

Table of Contents

DARK ROOM

ANOTHER WAY OF TELLING

APOTHECARY

Blue Grapes

There were days made entirely of dust
months of counter-winds

     and years unbalanced on the windowsill.

The soup poured in the same yellowed cup.

Newspapers appeared like oracles on your doorstep—
gilded fragments of anonymous love.

     You stayed in bed, read novels, drank too much.

God visited, delivered ice cream; returned your delinquent library books.

Is it simpler after you're dead
to watch the living like characters on an old-fashioned TV set?

     The dying are such acrobats—

You see them ringing doorbells with their clipboards
remarking on the globes of lilacs.

     They try to lure you out; request a drink of water,
some blue grapes. This does not work.

     Then the dying leave you to yourself—

to the girl dressed in black, suffused with commas,
and question marks——

     How to write your one blue life?

Tunnel

The wind blows through
the chain-linked yards of Allston Street.

It lifts the neighbor's forsythia into a Ferris wheel

of light and tips the girl aloft for the first time.

Now the petals follow her
along the cellar stairs in a yellow yelp

of March, passing the candy dish, filled
to overflowing by invisible hands—

ominous bullseyes, endless M&M's;
to the first floor tenants newly married;

the glamorous man with a green anchor
on his arm

renames her "pea-nut" and drives diesel trucks,
which excites the child, tremendously.

In the wind tunnel, now their living room,

the couple talk as if they live
among horses and lobsterpots.
                    As they embrace her,

she knows this is the encyclopedia

of her real world. The life of undershirts
and pipe smoke,

penny candy. Love so fresh it appears
palpable.

The wind of her heart now

follows her up more stairs to the other mother,
other father, then drifts down

hallways so grim it seems an aunt in Cincinnati
has just died

and then nine cousins drowned, too.

        The wind follows her through the attic of the dead
        where she touches their beautiful

chins with her thumb. It is peaceful here

when she walks through herself
        leaning above the current's edge.

There is No Substance
That Does Not Carry One Inside Of It

The real story is that she is a piece of light.
The real story is that light turns to flame
Turns to ember, then ash of burned
Sagebrush and city. The real story is
Sebastian remains behind to save the black
Mare with a bucket, a spiraling circle
Of stones. No one believes the real story
When the strangers politely repeat fire, state evacuate,
Stress *please*. Instead the hotelier at the front desk spits
Foreigners. Demands credit cards, passports, car keys.
Curses the tourists who create work after midnight;
Curses Isabella and the ships she sent out to sea
Which leads the man to look up past the courtyard,
The mountains ringed with fire beads, the little
Flames clearly flirtatious, clearly, beyond belief.

The Self

harmonizes when the world is quiet

takes early morning walks
along the curve of Puget Sound,

eavesdrops on bald eagles and eight-wheelers—

sometimes plays around.
No tax collector can find her

no private detective uncover her film-noir face.

The self wants only what she wants:
a hint of wasabi under the tongue

an outlaw's truth, a tumultuous embrace.

The self offers herself by the hour,
watches old musicals, whodunits—

only travels by train.

When the rain halts her solo
a double-note brings her home again.

She's a cameo of grit and glee

at home in lunar visions—
a grey plumed hat, a cinematic sheen.

History of a Kiss

And, if they are lovers—
is this the first kiss

or their mother's final
sparkling sorrow?

The children with their hats
cast down

cannot recall
the man's calm eyes, his animal

coat but all their lives
the taint of his cologne—

cinnamon and thyme—
will keep them

seeking love's illusions,
committing all its crimes.

Childhood Study: Fires Late August

Awake in the middle of the night,
we listen to the grass crackle, to the new world of evacuate.

Like monkeys we screech as the trees go pop—

yellow candelabras, we see and then not.
Now danger damages our capillaries

for the first time, the ladder trucks and sirens

seem like small toys compared with
the neighbor's fire-fangled trees.

What lit-up between us that summer—

three sisters clustered like barn cats— I can't say
except for a time camaraderie

warmed the soles of our feet, our robes

remaining intact just one season—
before it burned away.

Clouds, Begin Here

It is so hard to say what the dead really want.

In the lost fires of the notebook, words stumble

down the columns of green and white paper.

In the notebook of the unknown index, blank

description, we lose our blue hours. Begin with forget

shore line, heart line, forgive me serum.

If we're lucky, the mind sits up straight

in our interior tree house, our house of sky,

the remodeled one-car garage. Open the suitcase

of ink and erasures; let language spill out

in midair. Between ferryboat and bicycle,

between daybreak and meteor shower,

we create something holy:

apples and crackers and quiet.

Date

Instead of your St. Christopher medal
I finger a souvenir penny
from Seattle's Museum of Flight.

NASA's shuttle lifts off, suspended
in a tiny copper sky—
one zigzag line poised between

two revved-up rocket engines.

Abraham Lincoln's head
is reclaimed in service to space-age
travel. Nothing survives intact

of the coin but this:
BERTY — forgetting its L – I.

I press a second coin for you
though your name is neither Berty,
nor Christopher, nor Abe; touch it

to the openness of your palm.
In the vast space
of this moment, I offer a fractured

flight map from the creased
atlas of the mind. Before
the quadrille of a thousand

kisses have launched
as x's—before cotton
shirts unbutton or sky blue

jeans fly off—I ask for this:

Let our celestial travelers
revive in me that aerial
quiver of the green unknown.

Let the breath and spoon of it—
the unsupportable craters
and lakes of it— convince me

of the uncertain safety of the coupled dome home.

Embellishing the Picture

Surely there are islands of fiction
floating through the real to reel

projections of my days.
A hummingbird hovers

glimmering above the witch hazel,
a handsome camel, musically

inclined, hums in a cornfield
flummoxed by time.

Nothing extraordinary as the beach glass
and the fog-split sky

amp up this summer brightness
along the clefts of Cattle Point Drive.

Each day, or not each day,
we are alive: wing-tipped

gargoyles, rosehips, pink slips.
Nothing exceptional

in the ferryman's invitation to
please return to your car doors,

pelvic floors, back seats, geographies.
Why choose to live this one life

reluctantly? Instead, take this man
with the dimples out to dinner, take him

home to where new constellations
float above tiled rooftops.

To where the moon, just watered,
arrives at your front door.

Naming It

As a child I never believed in my name, never
lived as a Susan under the skin.

I struggled to master the double-spin of the S,
had no intention of becoming reptilian.

But how to resist such a field guide of letters?

I would study the tall girls
mouth the opulence of Kimberly, Kathryn, and Geraldine—

knew they would enter the world
wearing long lace dresses, never lost without an umbrella for the rain.

Unknown to me then was Susa,
ancient city of Persia, spot where Esther, orphaned, became queen.

Soon I shifted to Hebrew lily, Arabic lotus, rose—

sauntered towards スーザン in Japanese.
In the land of Malayalam, Shoshamma sang

Hello! then sailed further on than the outer Hebrides.

In Hungary, I made love like Zsuzsanna, Sana in Greek,
seduced Suzana in the blossoming tongue of Portuguese.

My signature looped round and round.

There were parabolas of lovers, the leaning tower,
ever-growing autographs of women and men.

When I left, the ship floated her S curves, dazzling

the knot, the hiss, the stratocumulus—
calling my name through the watery sky.

American History

Someday soon I'll be saying, at school

there were chalkboards, at school
we read books made of paper,

we drank milk from small cartons. We drew.
At school we met children unlike us,

studied evolution, enjoyed recess, plenty of food.

At school we made globes of papier-mâché,
built solar systems democratized in sugar cubes.

At school we sang harmonies of Lennon -
McCartney, we were cool;

collected pennies for children in
Biafra, Bangladesh, and Timbuktu.

There were teachers of Plato, King,
and Kennedy all paid for by taxpayers

supporting an ordinary American school.

Geography IV

Of what is the earth's surface composed?
                Elizabeth Bishop, *Geography III*

The world is a little place— a feather, a pebble, a spoon;
it turns to the left and taps its foot, a soldier signaling

to the rest of its platoon. The world doesn't know
it's a little world, thinks it's Greta Garbo in her Paris debut.

Watch as the world decorates half moons and cinnamon stars,
slips the Sound some islands to improve a stellar view.

Tonight the world wishes to sing what it means
to miss New Orleans; listens to the drowned hymns

of the Tchoupotulas while waiting on help,
recompense, a cat with umpteen kittens. Now the globe

pulls round again, scattering meaning along gold
rings of ramekins; a wizard of chemical breathing.

When invited to a soiree by this parched world,
down the Pinot Grigio while your inner life implodes

knowing nothing is as serene as it seems— the past
lit with menthol cigarettes; our futures just as unclean.

Andalucía

Occasionally, we start from scratch.

A new roadway, a country, a woman
who commands us, *miramé.*

We travel roundabouts as if they might
teach us to negotiate

cloud caravans out of the city,

out of the rhythm of doorframes
accompanied by Lorca

postcards and *Nights at the Alhambra* tea.

      *

I want to give you
syllables you can eat: tapas

of local tomatoes touched with ephemeral cheese;

oranges and lemon fruit
the size of scabby babies.

For you, I will silence the mourning doves

and offer the tilt-a-whirl of swifts
lifting up and out of the pepper tree.

And although I cannot gloss the language

of porn stars
for you, I'll purchase flash cards

of post-modern anatomy.

*

The night was cracked

and there were motionless salamanders;
the red signals of the Fiesta

lighting the windshield and the water
spray from your body.

As you squatted before the A7, before the great tankards of gin,

the world was yours.
A quirk of moonlight in the queendom.

Abstract

after a painting by Julie Aldridge

Perhaps the painter's angry
with her art—the ocean—the gallery—
  a comprehension that arrives too easily;

or is this simply Irish weather; a stormscape
well-lived in unsettled blues, long
undercoat of grey? What could it mean

that I look and can't see? Perhaps
there is no such thing as clarity.
In the middle ground, for instance,

an oblong labyrinth of mustard seed
or hay rolled tight, promise of
a light unfurling, a light you work to see.

Love Study in Nature

Listen, to walk on this lake is simply practice,
the sugaring of the fern fronds,
an entertainment in this evening's quickening snow.
And although I may look incomplete—
a broken sundial, an untapped toe—
I lie here beside you relearning
how to rise like a screech owl—

how to wing it. I leave behind
the forest of my past's past
and reclaim this drum roll—upbeat unknown.
Love, watch me, as we show ourselves, go
beyond deer paths, frozen fog, the bomber moon—
and know that my love is unsustainable.
And know that I do not know.

ANGLE OF APPROACH

Dear Self

The word I object to in the poem is blue
as in aquamarine, periwinkle, cornflower;

the shade of rain, of wind, of a girl's bicycle
stolen from the beach last July. I object

to the semi-colon; the commonplace
comma, the dash—as in Blue Danube—

blue fool—the sheen of a junkyard cat.

I object to the monogamous couplet

the iambic flash,   the turn
in the line like a magician who displays his jackrabbit

sheer entertainment done strictly for cash.
I abhor the smooth paper, the *vision fine* pen,

the hand mixing the ink, yes, even the author
who praises acres of tulips, orgasms in France.

Invention of Everything Else

Once a man offered me his heart like a glass of water,
how to accept or decline?

Sometimes all I speak is doubt

delineated by the double lines
of railway tracks; sometimes

I'm an incomplete bridge, crayon red Xs extending

across a world map.
A man offers me his bed like an emergency

exit, a forklift, a raft.

The easy-to-read instructions
sequestered in the arms of his leather jacket.

Sometimes a woman needs

small habits, homegrown salad, good sex.
Instead, she cultivates cats and a cupcake maker,

attempts enlightenment— prays to leaf skeletons on her deck.

The woman and the man say yes —
say no, say maybe, perhaps.

Neither one knows what they will do
to the other.

Perhaps they're acorns falling

on the roof, a Sunday paper, this all-embracing
ocean view.

Once a man offered his fortune
in drumbeats and song

tuned to some interior window; something buried in blue.

Never Simple

It was the simplest way to know one another—
to bring arms and legs together under white
sheets on a white mattress. To lay ourselves
leg to leg, breast to breast and retell our lives
as if the belief in words: one steadily drawing
another across a clean map could save us.
Yet once the meridians broke, the compass
rose curled under, what was left?
Nothing simple for men, nor women
as the lamplights flicker on, as the night planes flame
overhead. What is it that lovers need? The coordinates
for Timbuktu, the legend of its star dunes?
At dawn, may we push beyond milk and eggs, body crawl
to the Sahara's edge, to where it might be possible for us to ...

Life Study: College Love Poem

It was not about lobsterpots or advent calendars;
we were already schooled in the absurd—
 abandoned kittens fed with rubber tubes,

studying *The Miller's Tale* in the middle of the night,
take-out dinners of cold pizza and phad thai.
We asked, *why? Why grow up? Why love one*

or another? We flirted with death,
with Sexton or Plath, with the ineffable
arcing within us like highlights on a map.

We saw suicide as sexual, the girl on the second floor
who hung up her life: brilliant, quiet—
did it from her closet—visiting day

before the parents arrived. Better to travel
through *The House of Mirth* into happy hour,
kiss Eduardo by the Blue Wall, dance to The Doors.

When we stopped speaking, who was to blame?
A saltshaker heart? A stargazing brain?
Our plan: to become lunatics or lovers,

to live a thousand and one lives; to remain undercover,
remain Bedouins, or odalisques, or liars—
remain skeptical, and stubborn, and survive.

Hotel Strange in 103°

In the morning, Sebastian waters
the gravel and then, who knows why,

circles his hose round the oleander—
humming, he repeats the task.

After curling over the balcony,
the pepper tree looks as if

it *might* know. Perhaps the branches
communicate with the sea—

or don't, who can say
if Philipp photoshops wearing boxers,

if Benjamin composes his Irish
Symphony, as he implies, in the nude.

Dinner, is included—
a measure of unmistakably grey

food. Mackerel casserole
or mushroom? Who can say

why the Serbian shaves her head
or if the German is *really* in love?

Perhaps, this is what purgatory is like—
the taste of ash and of flowers,

the long approach to what we meant to say.

Mojacar, Spain

42

Here Are the Photographs
Taken When We Were Alive

Here are the photographs of the fire, peach-colored and pleasing.
Here are the mountaintops, the houses in the distance, orchards
Caught in the cross breezes. Here are the helicopters heard
All around us — appearing like over-fed birds dragging their
Bird-baths of water. Here are the fire trucks filling-up near the fountains.
The army, the Red Cross, the chaotic hum. Here snap, here click.
Hail the award-winning images.

The Burning Bush

The evacuation was as long
as a mountain range, as an S

curved beachside drive—
as the ash-strewn carriageway to Almería.

Ordinary objects we rescued

from extraordinary events,
like light bulbs pulled from a body—

What if it were better
not to speak of it

in Spanish or English?

＊

There was an orange hotel of angels
the size of an armada, 5 Stars,

where the firemen flirted and ate well.
There was a town christened

for monkfish and for olives.

Between the ocean and the mountain,
we practiced the adrenalin alarm—

played badly at search and rescue.
Ahora, por favor

saved by Sasson's newly invented iPhone.

*

Kissley orders that no one speak of the fire
that follows us—

the burning bush. Instead, she demands to tour

the Alcazaba, buy blue ice lollys,
drink punch.

She commands a flame-free life.

To relearn the difference
between suitcase and home.

Dutch Courtyard

after a painting by Max Liebermann

She labors, but at what she cannot know
for sure. She is alone, but does she know

how she's observed? The outer wall, the window
where girls of ivory and rose watch knowingly

above a makeshift fence; they can't
foresee the story of her winged back, know

nothing of the image-maker's script, the color work—
her supporting bit as laundress, lover, know-

it-all in service to the day's grey socks. Her face
remains defiantly obscured. What can she know

of art? She is arms—green bucket—angled foot—
headscarf—house dress—body of a woman. Knowledge

that she would most likely like to wash away—what good
will it do her? Blue motion of her life elevated to nowhere.

She's judged simple, dirty, ugly—and maybe so.
But see this future person standing here, knowing

all she does of sorrow, bend to palm the frame,
stung by something the world cannot express: the notion

of a second soul. She journeys in, traveling by window—
worker, rich girl, artist in the street: go beyond the known.

In a Village West of Galway

A woman takes her place
at the desk, a Moleskine open
before her like an eye.

She works, she pays, she cajoles
observation, determined to earn
the lighthouse within her—

and lead it to the page.
Yet how to transcribe
this invisible boundary line—

both lucid and in shadow;
to know her life? And step outside.
Linger where the debris

of language, unmoored,
accumulates as local bird
song, kite string, tossed-away

paradox. Her mind
navigates only this much—
images accumulate like buttons

in a button jar; needled
and threaded. Suspended—
she closes the journal, the world, the vastness—

tilt-a-whirls herself into the laundry
and lunchboxes. Cooking oil heating
from early-morning food stalls,

last evening's rain on pine needles,
cloudscapes that slip from lavender
into grey. Tomorrow she will

reattach herself, line by line-
break to this radiant quarrel,
this pocket-sized, revolutionary pen.

Manservant

A measure for the eyes, yes; pleasant enough
to fluff the pillows, suggest the season's wine;

to stand in dust-free attention, his gaze
taut as a tomcat economically hunting

his prize. The thing is, we are here
in the 21st century, outside the drawing

room, outside our everyday lives.
He appears as if by happenstance, Italian suit,

killer shoes, collar open to a sensual vee.
The wanton ways he knows reveal

themselves in his laughter—
a slice of falsetto both giggle and guttural,

a wilder life, slow on armchairs and pie.
Picture his profile in art house close-up—

the immigrant hero saving the planet
with a sweep of well-manicured hands

instead of Patrick, servant of Skibereen,
secure only in the graveyard shift

where beyond blue window sconces
the silver spokes of his ride disappear

low muffler caught up in song.

Lis Ard, County Cork

49

Weathervane

We are smack in the middle of the story:

in the middle of Mojacar
at midday
when the air hangs down like a woman's underwear—

violet and strong.

I am in the middle of a life,
midpoint of the year: July
when the radio plays halfway through the tango—

a middle pancake gone wild.

We don't know how to advance
or retreat.
Praise be to the center of the novel

before the crescendo—

before the hero begins to unwind.
The second teacup in a row of three
untethered from the port of departure

or the future's shore.

Not the fruit's rind
or its sweet seed
but the flawed heart's core.

In this Galaxy of Seeing How Much Remains Unseen

Branches of *almost* balance with leaves of *not quite*—
Out-of-body afternoons pinned to evenings of ringtones
not ringing; holidays with a single red plate

and an internet offer of men. *Dear blank, it's not
too late* to meet extraterrestrials, practice alchemy,
resurrect a lost dress size. Or stay.

Yet, what to say of the shimmer and the lace
after the fact; the upside-down heart stained
with the lover's hands? How ephemeral

this leaving, like music under the air—
gilding the past—that double-headed antelope—
repeating *it happened* in bright circular parades.

Is this what you wanted?
An arm slipped under your waist while you slept?
And still, how this galaxy of scars—

signals above us in blue transparent space.

Life Study: Camellias

We need to look outside
ourselves to see

the sloping heads, the cartography of light

along the lip
of a hammered copper tray.

What might white camellias say

in such a private
disheveled state?

So much, we know,

belies the flounce of petals
in a tall, white vase—

a midlife meditation—

heaven-spent,
like bodies after sex

before one falls away.

Visitation

after a painting by Edgar Degas

Two sisters, look sexy in black dresses,
as if they've just returned from a funeral

and are now ready for salvation through art.

The shy one presses the guidebook to her chest:
maps, odd facts, and history

the curator recounts, as if Monsieur knows

the artist's vision best.
The beautiful sister scorns smart words

lifts her eyebrows beyond where I can see.

In the museum of their hearts
in a stream of baked gold leaf

the room's vanishing point betrays a haunting tranquility.

How to survive the well-lived life?

Trapped in their pockets lie the clues—
a tin of mints and the letter still unsent.

Darling, This Relationship is Damned

Dear Fire—

how you flirt and flicker,
you scat along

this Spanish seaside town;
hot lover, tango

dancer, who insists
on playing around.

Yes, I fear you— home
wrecker, double-crosser,

fickle fool made of gasses

and tongues.
Of course you persist

with your side of the
story: chemistry,

cigarettes, the late-night pleasures
of coffee with jam.

Am I wrong to even write?

Wildfires hugging
the roundabouts, the hillsides—

Count them: eight hours
before the little trucks arrived.

It's not my fault, you'd pout,
and yes, you could be right.

Certain unforgivable elements conspire—
intense heat and dust and men.

Natural for a flame to grab
what it wants, whether

lemongrove, or nightclub, or sin.

You Who No Longer Concern Me

I revise the canvas of an under painted sky

move the shoreline backwards until blank.
But how to erase the island countries—

the sea-filled nights, your love sighs more

addictive than cheap flights? I am tired
so tired of small fights, the sleepless pacing, waking

the cats up, the damned neighbors, the fucking

flies. I am ready for another life: blue
lawn afternoons with roundtable friends—

jasmine, mint cocktails, a full vegetable bed.

You who no longer concern me, you are
the unread novel, the half-closed eye, the rubato

of trains in this city's west section.

And if you were to ask me now
with shimmering bees, scat film-strip

jazz and endnote: *Will you be mine?*

I do not believe that it would be enough—
but you may try to right our lives again.

You may try, but I am unconcerned.

The World No Longer Resembles Itself

We've been through catastrophe together
and it shows. Now we are the regulars

with melted suitcases and smoke-pearled
skin. We drink casually with the owner's

avuncular friends, speak avalanched lines
of a local language—our gaze

locked on the half-charred pueblo:
the roof tiles, the wounded lemon groves.

Purloined with the pure after-fact
of fear, I consider the burnt

pomegranates, the charred almonds
in fire-proof cups, the f-ing napkins.

For now, we are displaced persons;
we are credit cards considering long-necked cervezas

because we can, can watch the community
reassemble in a studio pose—

the suited-up little honchos, the hair-sprayed
boy reporters. You note their glam—

the silk ties and sharp teeth outside our window.
They report to us from the world

across the road and again, above the bar
by the hotel's only phone. Our pueblo's

declared "disaster zone" and the ads for detergent
follow. Our shirts will never come clean.

Darling, listen as the barman strums flamenco—
Now, before we somehow rise and go.

DARK ROOM

Tricks a Girl Can Do

Hannah Maynard was one of the first professional women photographers in Victoria, British Columbia. After the death of her teenage daughter, Lillie, she created a series of multiple exposure self-portraits. From 1884 to 1896, Maynard's work grew progressively eccentric.

I will hang myself in picture frames
in drawing rooms where grief
is not allowed a wicker chair

then grimace back at this facade
from umbrella eyes
through a cage of silvering hair.

Look! I've learned to slice myself in three
to sit politely at the table
with ginger punch and teacake;

offer thin-lipped graves
of pleasantries. I develop myself
in the pharmacist's chemicals

three women I'm loathe to understand—
presences I sometimes cajole
into porcelain light and shadow.

We culminate in a silver gelatin scene—
a daughter birthed from a spiral shell,
a keyhole tall enough to strut through.

The Key to Unraveling in Plain Sight

after a multiple exposure self-portrait, late 1880s

Unsettling how Hannah stares back
at me, holds the empty saucer

skyward as if she recognizes her own riddle of release.

Then she overlaps the images and leaves
no line of separation

but splits herself open like a magic trick;

now she's Hannah times three.
Desolate as a drawing room

with no sorrows left to bear;
a severed body (hung

in a golden frame, floating on tired air).

She pours her tea rather gleefully
on second Hannah's head.

And does not regret it. Does not,

does not, does not allow
Lillie to stay dead.

Dieffenbachia Photo Gem, 1884

She began to create her Gems of British Columbia—hundreds and then thousands of children's little faces interlocked in greeting cards, in diamond wreathes and abalone shells.
—Claire Weissman Wilks

The parlor plant's been camouflaged
with photo gems of children:
leaves enhanced with cutout infants,

toddlers and the doe-faced world
of adolescents. Where the dirt
would be expected, more tintypes

of Victoria's privileged youth
grin like modern gargoyles
montaged with simple glue.

You need more
than a microscope to see
the seven leaves with seven years

of Hannah's only picture plant.
Faces infused as an orchestra
of phantoms, of innocents scored in time.

Dumb cane.
Mother-in- law.
Inflorescence.

Endless Forms, Most Beautiful

after a multiple exposure self-portrait of Hannah Maynard, c.1894

So she keeps her herringbone hands busy with teacups and white flowers
and murmurs to no one what she will create. No nephew sawed in half

will interest her today, no devoted husband measuring buttes
but a suitcase of her own bright follies. The living room pulses on

and off with gunpowder expertly fitted for her flash. Or perhaps
the room becomes a kind of snowbound mausoleum exhibiting her grief

one winter afternoon. (It is quite impossible to know, but let's presume.)
No more inner voices to wake her from sleep, no more fussy wives

who arrive with meat pies and then hurry their bosoms home
to living daughters. In the frame, Hannahs stand here, sit there, bend over

to brush a bouquet of lilies from another Hannah's hair.
From house left and then house right, solitary Hannahs float like smoke

rings into me. I should have known — the artful dodge, her concentric days,
unwavering dark-sky stare — recognized my own pathology.

Strange Symmetry of Past, of Present

after a self-portrait set in a keyhole: late 1890s

Actually, the past does slip forward
through a keyhole,

alive, feeding on our half-
recounted facts and figures,

penny-farthing bicycles and pancake
breakfasts annually eaten.

How we learn to study it
in private (the past)

like reading the phrasing
of rare birds or fisherman

sweaters or scat; to unlock
the world in retrospect —

a human kind of heaven.

Take photography, for instance.
Here the 19th century returns

as Hannah poses herself
in crisp black and white:

She's made a negative space
on the threshold of a life-

sized paper cut-out: keyhole
fit for the movie sets

of Orson Welles (well before
Orson was born).

Her figure stands neither in
nor out of the century but floats.

She's her own avant-garde parade

a riddle, amulet, sunflower seed;
comic, crazy, genius woman

finding the multiplicity of things—

patterns of desire across a face:
two dead daughters, ghost light, and similar fates.

The Tangible, Intangible

after a self-portrait of Hannah Maynard, multiple exposure c.1894

Afterwards, she surveys the site:
the jostled cups, a buffalo rug,
backdrop of bookcase

overstuffed with trompe l'oeil painted spines.

The sound of the photograph
would be island rain
and the animal cry of the child gone—

In the darkroom she works alone

cajoles waterfalls, brings to light
the floating picture frame,
the doily's difficult knowledge—

Commonplace days she survives
with a mirror trick, a few glass plates
that echo *don't let go; let go.*

Hannah, Decanter, and Cloud

self portrait at 74

Age is still decanters on the table
the size of small chandeliers
or cloud foam. You, remember,
are the one that is unmade
as of yet, unknown. Medium
merely to an image, a woman

studio-posed. Self-portrait
developed for the afterlife—
our ticker-tape world

of tableaus and combs
circling on. And. Then. Somehow
your barnacled vessel
lit from within like a carriage
clock or sea-washed amber stones.
Have you been taken?

the Victorians inquired; from flesh
into silver salts, into gaslight paper
or gold? Everyone becoming older.

Your gaze darts forward, lifts
beyond the mayor's clapperboard
home, the dead dove, the séance, the bones.
One unknowable instant—
even as the aperture quietly
holds, even as the light

decants over gloved hands
that turn into clouds.
Don't tell me this is only a story.

Tell me there's more to our lives
than jigsaws and doorknobs,
more than tumbleweed, sediment or sex.
We live for the tunnel, the years signatured
together into the surreal, for our art
imperfect and striving.

ANOTHER WAY OF TELLING

Sugar, You Know Who You Are

You who carry the sky in your hands
open to the world as peach pie;

you who harmonize like a Miracle,
a Temptation, a Spinner, a Top—

What record shop or percussive bop
did you swing from? What city

plot did you rhythmically cajole
of a singer making music to a woman—

not young, not yet so old! Remember?
We watched ourselves

as if watching strangers improvise
a summer's afternoon

composed from the riff of madrona
leaves, iced coffee, and a public wading pool.

Maybe we were beginning our lives
together, maybe.

The hinges squeaked
a kind of jazz tune—coconut bars

and jelly rolls, Boston egg creams,
and red velvet stars. No longer

strangers now, the blue gates open
at dusk and look

here you are: infusing the globe
in rhythms, sugaring our nights with sparks.

Stories from Strange Lands

I tell you my lovers never last—
I'm serious, but my sincerity

sparks laughs. You read me
over the telephone lines

reportage from tonight's bath:
If God = love (+ 1 yogic breath)

then it's best to locate our days
fucking in a feather bed.

This is an ecstatic theology
we heartily agree on—

a praxis that's not half bad.
But what I really want

to offer, my beloved,
is news from another land.

When a good man, a worker—
a trapeze artist or Cleveland dad—

becomes injured, the French believe
it merely deepens his craft,

artistry entering the body
with a dangerous leap or a fall.

The story makes of mistakes
something holy. My first near miss

of your kiss, your undisclosed desire
for reading trash. Our skill set working

as we continue our lives
over a landscape of scars and of mishaps.

Cloud Pharmacy

How many apothecary drawers
could I fill with these deliberations?

The pharmacist's paper cone
parsing out a quarter cup

of love's resistant drug,
spoons measuring new prescriptions

for my uncertainty, heartsway, gesture.
Give me cobalt bottles

leftover from aunt iska's cures,
albastrons of ointments, resins to resolve

the double-helix of desire inside of me.
Where is the votive, the vessel,

the slide rule calculation—
of how much good love

alchemically speaking
is good enough?

I want spindrift nights on swimmer's
thighs. I want an Egyptian

elevator inlaid in camphorwood and ivory;
a West African drumbeat, an eggnog, a god.

I want waves and summer all year long.
I want you. And I want more.

Letter to M

If I could, I would protect you from your own sorrow.
From the frayed ends of welcome mats, the crush of 5 AM

traffic, maple trees and the stock market's long descent.
I would shelter you from mortgaged rooms that open

inward and deflect the day's inglorious path to pill-filled
nights; pensioners along the promenade, the foghorn's

amorous cry. Mostly, I would harbor you from appetites
old—young—your hopes rife as wildfire to disarm

any woman for an hour, a tryst never more
than an ottoman away. In Thailand, they say a generous

heart is a water heart, but today tears don't come that way.
You say *I can't make love without music,* as if this were revelation

made into art — praise song to what rhythm your body prays.

The Tide-Tables Foretold the Future in Our Hands

Perhaps

happiness begins when we take ferries—

the portholes and crowds

and popcorn

of our lives lifting them-

selves enthusiastically forming a map

inked in revisions

of Tuareg blue. Or we become

a midsummer season, ginko cloud

cover, savored

best from the eyebrow of the storm.

You'd say we're more like a window-

seat, the unexpected

upgrade, the stranger's gaze: what we

so rarely risk or breathe.

My questions appearing

like sea lions—each arc and bow

a new illusion—

                  salt-skin arcing, then releasing

in the peculiar light of minnows

spiraling out to herringbone pools

                  re-ordering why—rethinking how?

Conundrum

I spend the night deciding whether to break in two
like two halves of a muskmelon split open.

I spend my days wondering if I am married

or single, puzzling out the simplest things
(I should really know).

I take mornings, take centennials,

to choose a camelback sofa or a Barcelona chair
as if décor resolves the conundrum

of lives jig-sawed together

or remaining lonely as brooms.
How do I knot my tie?

To live in coupledom we must wrestle

our omissions imprecisions.
Am I a woman or a man?

Should I zip up jeans in *junior miss*

or choose the cheaper tag in third floor *boys?*
O why must we feign a choice

between single malt and chiffon pie

except to bring this quest
to its confusion?

We are bound / we are cleaving / we are bi.

Perhaps You Are—

Perhaps you are late
to work or on your way
to an afternoon

in bed with your blue
eyed, fine-boned
faithless lover.

Navigating the cobble
stone, you walk
alleyways stained

in nameless molds
and young men's
urination games.

Your body takes in
the court, The White
Horse, the florid market

place with its balcony
of exiled clocks, Slavic
clogs and unloved

lacquered canes planted
like question marks
along the filigreed gates.

Today, you are
not unhappy.
So when it comes—

precise as flight
a lifting beyond
anything you've known—

what can you do
but accept this fragment
unfolding out of the sky:

You will live
this life alone—
And you will write—

Lancaster, England

After Shiva

To mark the end of Shiva, mourners take a short walk around the neighborhood as a way of taking a first step back into the world. It is believed the deceased abides with the mourners.

Here, under a tide of clouds,
bamboo lining the yard—
fronds fold into winter like the crowd
of well-wishers after your death—
bending and nodding
promising to call, to come back—
noodle pudding and all
those stewed fruits. The neighbors
and double cousins kissing and gone
over the balcony, sleepwalking
into laundry and mailboxes,
past the blue bucket hanging
from the linden tree
(which the Irish use to signal home).
What does anyone remember of us?
A fist or a cry, a knife or a belt,
or a photograph from Kennebunkport,
your sunglasses larger than sand dollars.
Father, send me a message,
even one almond keening signals
the dead won't forget us,
that there's a ladder (perhaps on wheels)
which takes our souls away; takes us
as we recite the scores from
Sunday's Sox game or the price of plums
at Star Market. Divide up the days
and years you've been gone
and what will we find there—
a morning glory or a curse?
What light informs where we travel?
What depths of feeling keep us stumbling
on in anguish safe at home?

What Hodan Tells Me

For $80 you can become a Somali citizen
with a blue passport,
a diplomat for not much more.
The American Embassy woman confides,
"You are going to suffer culture shock
but *The Bold and the Beautiful* will help."
I thought I'd die by bullets
and then I thought I'd die by air.
If you can't be a mountain
attach yourself to one.

Anniversary

Where lives the language that fits us,
a place carved beyond pineapples

and pears where we may dwell?
Light questions the sky,

reflects back on the hourglass
and blue dress pooled on the floor.

What will it take to keep desire?
I'm wondering about the openings

in waffles and omelettes,
about the stations of the tongue;

nouns of the body: earlobes,
vertebrae, bums. How to rearrange

the sentences of myself, yourself;
ourselves wanting more—

the way the magnolia in August
resembles little of its former allure?

I'm searching out infinitives
in penny circulars for *to have* and *to hold*.

And here come the cats at a gallop
headed above us, over the headboard,

aware of our mutual banquet of crow.
I'm unearthing new modes for how

we'll roll on through orchestras of snores,
through searching out night guards

lost in the dark; through succor
and repair, through death let us part.

Cougar Ridge

The red squirrels sound their travel alarm,
bop their bodies, no smarter than small dogs.
Sometimes the world is all birdcall and breeze;
sometimes it's wild berries, a brindle moth.
Let August roam on another month
and if the universe complains, who cares?
Nothing to do but follow the trail, listen hard
as the madrones phone home, leaf up and disappear.
And what if we never went shopping again?
No breakfasts out or Monday nights at *The Rose?*
We'd gather, grow old, and I'd imagine, foolishly grin.
Like these kamikaze squirrels— count me in.

Port Townsend, WA

After, Ever After

She erases the phonebook, the *New York Times*,
empties each photo album,

bureau drawers of glass buttons and brassieres.

Now she deliberates the day
her beloved's name

repeats the word for lavender—*love in her*—
loved her. . .

She tries again in yesterday.

Mornings mistakes the Northern Flicker
for a cigarette, the smoke-filled bars

of flappers and the sky
like a Blue Hawaiian on the rocks.

Until everything becomes today—

pillbox and hourglass, Aricept
and the teapot's luminescence.

Brown Cows rising
into the forever—

night lights and all-night TV.

Going—

*Until one has loved an animal, a part of one's
soul remains unawakened.* —Anatole France

I photograph you every morning
In a cruel attempt to capture
A formal souvenir of what I love
After breakfast, and then
Each day a little less
You take a stand, examine finches
Windowpanes knocking
Your head against my hand
Until you don't—
There is no way to tell you
That you are going
With few days left
For what our rebel hearts relay

Faraway

I like it here in the green Beara chair
the Wellington boots

      perched in pairs beneath the kitchen window.

I like the palm trees so clearly out of place,

the Irish cow's peculiar baritone keening

like a mobile phone
           on pulse.

I like it here because the peninsula is curved and long,

the road edged in orange wildflowers and dung.

I like how the clouds put on a juried show
         and the rain.

That here the interior world opens
lightly as a letter

with no sentences of sorrow.

The World to Come

Let's say we make our own happiness, roll over
in the fields, stain our arms and legs with blue

grass; let's say there's simply one year left
to draw lists of clouds, slip guilt free through bars

of chocolate, hold each other in this black hole
of restlessness. This life.

Tonight we will battle the linoleum squares,
laundry stairs, glass deck where one day

the body is sure to grab its last hungry breath.
What if all that's left for us is gravity,

canned soup, a shimmer of thinning hair?
Let's say we make our own happiness even so—

the tail swoop of katsura trees, triple shots
of strong coffee, a folded map—

Then may I remember to thank the academy
of daily minutiae: suitcases, car keys, a friend's

first novel of karaoke. Who says we can't
have it all: the house of sky and soft catcalls—

Who says we can't find another way
to fail, to come up short, to catch and release.

Notes and Dedications

"Blue Grapes" pays homage to the line "the dying are such acrobats" from the poem, "Trapeze," by Deborah Digges.

"Clouds, Begin Here," is inspired by Stephanie Kallo's novel, *Sing Them Home*. This poem is dedicated to her generosity of spirit.

The poem "Andalucía" borrows the following line from Federico Garcia Lorca, *The night was cracked and there were motionless salamanders*. This poem is dedicated to Kimberly Campanello.

"Date," "Stories From Strange Lands," and "Sugar, You Know Who You Are" are dedicated to Jeff Wasserman. "Sugar, You Know Who You Are" borrows its first line from Rainier Maria Rilke.

"Invention of Everything Else" borrows its title from Samantha Hunt's selfsame novel and one half of its first line from the poet, Eduardo Corral.

"Life Study: College Love Poem," is for Pam Loring.

"The Burning Bush," and "Here are the Pictures Taken When We Were Alive" are dedicated to Kissley Leonor and Jeremiah Sasson Fryer. The title of the latter comes from Carolyn Forche's poem, "Nocturne" in her book, *blue hour*.

"Dutch Courtyard" is after *Dutch Courtyard*, 1882, Max Liebermann, in the Founders' Collection of the Frye Art Museum, Seattle, WA.

"A Village West of Galway," is dedicated to Geraldine Mills.

"Life Study: Camellias" is after *Roses*, 1895, by Soren Emil Carlsen, in the Founders Collection of the Frye Art Museum, Seattle, WA.

"Visitation" is after *Visit to a Museum*, Edgar Degas, c.1879-1890, permanent collection of Museum of Fine Arts, Boston, MA.

The title "In this Galaxy of Seeing How Much Remains Unseen," is a revision of a line by James Elkins from his book, *The Object Stares Back*, Mariner Books, 1997.

The title "The World No Longer Resembles Itself," is after a painting by Katherine Porter in the permanent collection of the Portland Art Museum, Portland, OR. The poem is based on experiences in Mojacar, Spain, during the wildfires of August 2009.

Hannah Maynard (1834-1918) was born in Cornwall, England and immigrated to Canada, eventually settling in Victoria, B.C. in 1862. From the late 1880s to the mid 1890s, Maynard created a series of self-portraits experimenting with multiple exposure and trick photography shots. These images often show three or four Hannahs in the same frame. Thanks to Claire Weismann Wilks for her book on Maynard's work, *The Magic Box — The Eccentric Genius of Hannah Maynard*, Exile Editions, 1980.

The poem, "Endless Forms, Most Beautiful" owes a great debt to the poem "Murder Mystery" by Katharine Whitcomb. The poem's title is a line by Charles Darwin, as told to me by Catherine Barnett. "Endless Forms, Most Beautiful" is also the title of a poem by Barnett from her award-winning collection, *Game of Boxes*, Greywolf Press, 2012.

"The Tangible, Intangible" contains a line inspired by Pippa Little's poem "Hope" found in her gorgeous collection, *Overwintering*, Carcanet Press, 2012.

"Cougar Ridge" is dedicated to Jan North, with great appreciation.

"Faraway" is dedicated to Sue Forbes and the writers in residence at Anam Cara Writers and Artists Retreat in the West of Ireland— past, present, and future.